WORDS OF LIFE

(AUTOBIOGRAPHY)

TANAYA BHALERAO

Dedicateed to

My Husband Sharad Bhalerao
Lakhamapur

Contents

Words of Life

(Autobiography)

Tanaya Bhalerao

PREFACE

"Firstly I thought what greatness do I have, that I have, that I have to tell anyone about? I live just like millions of people in this country; I have been crushing away with the hope that I could become free of my suffering but when I restudied struggles of Chhatrapati Shivaji Maharaj, Chhatrapati Sambhaji Maharaj their biographies, I collected tremendous inspirations in the battle of my life and finally I decided that I should share my personal experience for the motivation of millions of the people in our country and lastly I started narration of my autobiography."

Tanaya Bhalerao

19 Feb. 2022

Quote 1

"ARISE, AWAKE AND STOP NOT
TILL THE GOAL IS REACHED"

Swami Vivekananda

Quote 2

"HELPING HANDS ARE
BETTER THAN
PRAYING LIPS."

MOTHER TERESA

Quote 3

"DREAM is not what you see in
sleep,
DREAM is something which doesn't
let you sleep."

Dr. A. P. J. Abdul Kalam

Acknowledgements

I want to thank Respected Dr. Sudhir Deore Sir for editing this Book. Sir gives the most valuable finishing touch to the conents penned by me and performed an important role in showing this work the light of the day.

Thank you so much KDB Institute of Lakhamapur, My Husband Sharad Bhalerao and all staff of KDB.

Also thanks to Book cover artist Darshana Kolge and Notion Press Publication, Chennai.

Thanks my Mother and Father.

Thanking you again.

- Tanaya Bhalerao
Principal of KDB School
Lakhamapur - 423213

Book Cover : Darshana Kolge
Publication : Notion Press, Chennai
First Edition : 19 Feb. 2022
Price : Rs. 150

I

Birth and Infancy

1984 - Birth, 1985 - Infant:

23rd March 1984 was the day when my wonderful incredible story mean life journey was started. We women are sacred consider in India. Women are known here as goddess. They have been worshiping Goddess Durga for protection, strength and motherhood, Lakshmi for love, wealth and fortune, Parvati for power beauty and harmony and Saraswati for learning wisdom and knowledge.

My father a school teacher of Girnare high school who recently begot a daughter should be happy because a glim or glyph of Durga, Lakshmi, Parvati or Saraswati has already arrived in his house but I don't know why, he was worried may be nervous perhaps he had three other daughters too and I am fourth.

My mother who was house-wife was really delighted and cheerful because she is very responsible in all activities. I am like her and always try to imitate her in each and every activities during cooking, handling house holds and in small and big tasks her one of the extra ordinary works was that she did not treat us like a daughter but she always treated us like a sons this story is truly incomplete without the discussion about my lovable sisters Kalpana, Chetana, Seema and my parents kept my name 'Surekha'. My sisters were like my friends.

"Having a sister is like having a best friend you can't get rid of you know whatever you do, they still be there."

We were different flowers from father's garden we enjoyed a lot our childhood we made may times surprise trip to spend some quality time with mama and daddy. We also enjoyed in host a family meal by inviting our nearest and dear relatives at home. My happy house was home and it was as divine as temple.

"Everyone needs a house to live but a supportive family is what builds a home."

We were happy including some nuisance one of my aunts use to my mother that

"When will you beget a son?" only daughters are not enough for a family inheritance of property and success is a part of life so one at least one son is being necessary."

"धन आहे पण कण नाही वंशाचा दिवा नाही."

It's nature of these kinds of people but today boys and girls are not treated differently its old trends show inequality today we are aware of women's issued and inequality. It become glaringly clear to one when I was studying I also saw that women are regarded as less intelligent than men it is totally injustice with women here I want to share my personal experience with you that these kinds of people who always spread bias in society they are failed and unsuccessful in their life. Although today the University of Pune has renamed as "Savitribai Phule Pune

University and we still trapped or stuck in the gender inequalities.

Swami Vivekanand, let me share an experience or an incident of Swamiji with you.

Once an English man asked Swami Vivekananda.

"Why Indian ladies do not shake hands?" Swami Vivekananda replied him.

"Can an ordinary citizen shake hands with the Queen in your country?"

English man answered "No".

Then Swami told a historical quote.

"In our country each and every women similar to a queen."

These lines encouraged not only my mother but thousands of the mothers to fight against gender bias.

II

Infancy early childhood

1986 - 1987 – 1988 - 1989 :

Apart from all thee things one special and supportive plus sign for us was education. Out guardians were highly educated and qualified too. But society and people of our village all fingers are not equal so here my birth means

"मुलगी झाली हो: why does she beget a daughter instead of a son?

Its power of almighty gives daughter to someone and son to somebody but people always try to interrupt in the rule of nature, they try to distract us but should always be optimistic my mother was also an optimistic lady. She is today also optimistic and very struggling lady, she faced a lot of problems regarding medical deficiency and those days' people used to tolerate unavailability of medicine but my brave mother not only fought with medicine problems but also succeed and work in farm. She had spent usually her time with elder sister 'Mai' at the time people were through gentleman and real understanding between husband and wife as well as good mother.

लबो पे उसकी बददुआ नही होती
बस एक माॅ हैं जो कभी हमसे खफा नही होती

Yes, I am glad to say you, I am a strong woman because a very strong woman raised me.

इस दुनिया में बिना किसी स्वार्थ के
प्यार सिर्फ एक माॅ ही कर सकती है

'Mai' my elder sister helped her very much and other people also because at that time people were generous, polite, civil, well-mannered and through gentleman careful they usually would give countless respect to others specially a teacher of their locality, luckily or fortunately my father was also a best teacher. People gave him respect and we were prestigious family. My father used to teach us and used to tell us some sentences which are similar to given quote.

"If you lose wealth, you lose nothing,
But if you lose dignity and self respect,
You lose everything."

So our family was honestly prestigious due to these kinds of moralities. In the society we are well known because of my father here one proverb regarding my childhood I wan to share with you that

"लहानपण देगा देवा, मुंगी साखरेचा रवा."
"It's never too late to have a happy childhood."

My precious five years of early childhood including infancy was charming and I started my study at Zilla – Parishad (z-p) school at Gunjal Wadi. My Varhade ma'am is with my old memories. I always remember her as she magnanim and too kind for us.

**"BETTER THAN A THOUSAND
DAYS OF DIGNITY STUDY
IS ONE DAY WITH A GREAT
TEACHER."
JAPANESE PROVERB**

But in my point of view.

**"Thousands books are simply books but a
Teacher has ability to teach us.
Tanaya Bhalerao**

She (Varahde) is one of my favourite teachers too. One humorous discussion with you about those days, you know in those days floor built – up by using cow dung or cow manure. Some times me and two friends 'Rohini and Nandini' collected cow pats for repairing school floor, they studied and often come for masti in our village although they were cousins and I was only their friend but they loved and played with me as a sister.

It will be grievance if I will not narrate about my grandparents who loved me a lot I missed my mother so much when I lived with my grandparents but they were real compensation of my mother. I also love them because this memories give me too much pleasure and a plenty of happiness we were talking about Varahde ma'am afterward

I'll narrate about my grandparents too.

So I was wise student and gave a plenty of respect to my 'Varahde' ma'am and other teachers also. She belongs to Deola. We used to enjoy a lot. I remember her one song

"लाल टांगे वाले तेरा फेटा लाल लाल

तेरा चाबुक लाल लाल"

Not only me my friends, my family but my grandpa also liked this song.

I can't forget my memorable childhood, no life without childhood.

"If you carry childhood with you,

You will never - never

Become old."

"Bachpan ke din char, na aayenge baar baar.

Jee le, Jee le mere yaar, Jeb khaali to udhar Jee Zindagi

....

(Taare Zameen Par)

৪৩

III

Grandpa's house

1990-1992 (1ˢᵗ - 3ʳᵈ School days) :

As I portrayed that I will narrate about my grandparents, firstly I want to tell you that my loving grandparents looks after me and my sister Kalpana, as in advance I narrated about my elder sisters Kalpana, is one of them. Our primary education we took from Gunjal Wadi, Taluka Deola at Nashik district, really their true affection is unforgettable. They provided us food always on time and before time, new dresses on each and every festivals, my grandpa and his older brother 'Mothabhau' daily gave me 20 paise as pocket money for chocolates. I was a naughty girl, rarely share those things to Kalpana. She would always quarrel with me scolding me but apart from all these mischievous she used to help me during study and while cooking delicious food due to all of these it became my one of the favorite places.

Sarja (Mothabhau), my grandpa and his wife my grandmamma were nearly 70/75 years old but he was responsible one. They were eight brothers including him among them he was eldest. If I will talk with you about their personality you will be astonish. My grandpa was really optimistic, cheerful, dynamic and energetic personality but his example like coconut because I know him closely, although due to his energetic personality. All neighbors dare not to came in front of him but he was really exactly like a coconut or walnut hard, solid and brutal from out side and soft, simple and kind from inside.

My grandma was also comparable or same like him, she used to make Chapati and always cooked on 'Chul' (a kind of stove) but the food which she used to cook on chul were honestly delicious, tasty, full organic, hygienic and natural. They loved nature that is why nature also loved them a lot their thinking was natural.

"निसर्गाची काळजी घ्या
निसर्ग तुमची दामदुपटीने काळजी घेईल."

and today we should analyze our activities, malpractice is everywhere but we should not neglect theories of our forefathers even grandpa was a man of discipline and self – control but never made any type of dispute with others even not with my grandma. People afraid, apprehension by his appearance, his blue color kurti, white dhoti and Turban (pagadi) on head. My maternal – uncle 'MAMA' also afraid, apprehension to talk with him. It was the time of Chimney light at the evening it illuminated or lit – up. We called 'Chopalo' to it and we used at that time bullock cart. We enjoyed very much in our haveli type house. You know my grandpa was a hardworking person, he used his time skillfully in the construction of a vast and wide house including hall, rooms, area to play, place for washing clothes, kitchen, stairs with wonderful and obliging stair case I in fact it was really well planned house constructed by him. I remember we used to gather to play in our courtyard and ultimately it full of people. One extra room was there at the back side of our house although it was belongs to us but had given to labours.

I remained or remember those day and my civil, well-mannered and through gentleman grandpa too. I have plenty of respect for them.

"Don't underestimate the wisdom of ancestors."
African Proverb

IV

Secondary School life

1993 to 1999 (4th to 10th) :

I was motivated and encouraged by her. She kept thousands of inspirational and persuasive qualities. She is none of other but one and only my elder sister and she faced an exam of scholarship and passed. She suggested me too, here I tried but couldn't pass and she recommend me again to face it because she not only passed exam but awarded by honorable Mangesh Padgawakar sir this incident made my father very happy and encouraged me she always inspired me by saying that

मंजिल उन्ही को मिलती है जिनके
सपनो में जान होती है,
सिर्फ पंख होने से कुछ नही होता,
हौसलो से उड़ान होती है

These kinds of sentences she used to use for my bright dazzling future. From 4th to 10th standard I was with my parents. I lived in join family there was no enough time and lack of opportunity regarding the study. I used to go for study at my considerate and good tempered friend's house.

In 10th standard my strategy concerned study converted as crazy student who study a lot my 90% study I did at my good tempered friend's house. In 10th I solved 80 question papers without any help but here reward was not regards my expectation. I got 79% which made me unhappy may be it is in destiny. I never gave up I struggled for best outcome and for my bright, best dazzling future.

लहरो से डरकर नौका पार नही होती
कोशिश करने वालो की हार नही होती
नन्ही चीटी जब दाना लेकर चलती है
चढती दिवारों पर सौ बार फिसलती है
मन का विश्वास रगो में साहस भरता है
चढकर गिरना गिरकर चढना न अखरता है
आखिर उसकी मेहनत बेकार नही होती
कोशिश करने वालो की हार नही होती

☙

V

Higher Secondary School

2000 - 2001 (11th and 12th) :

After 10th I took admission at Malegaon KBH Science College, firstly I stayed in hostel there was not good atmosphere in concern of study and food was not also nutritious, poshtic even hygienic, that day I released,

> "ना जाने माॅं क्या मिलाया करती है आटे मे
> के घर जैसी रोटिया और कही मिलती ही नही !..."

I passed one embarrassed year in that hostel and 12th class I migrated in a bungalow of my friend Mansi (manshi) their standard of living high but simple they believed that the simple living and high thinking and help others are real goals of our life.

**"HELPING HANDS ARE
BETTER THAN
PRAYING LIPS."
MOTHER TERESA**

Although they were rich but not egoistic. They not only permitted me to spend time there but provide thousands of the facilities also. I missed my loving parents a lot and perhaps they too.

I faced hundreds of the difficulties during study and numerous unrest or troubles. I took tuition / guideline by several intuitive or mystical personalities. My Physics teacher in tuition was Patil sir, Chemistry by Shirode sir, Biology by Aanand Patil sir. I couldn't attend college lectures studied only in tuition till the last day of 12th we were in Mansi's room, me, Swati, Mansi lived together but I tried very much in 12th and it changed my life style goals of life too.

Study, hardwork, struggle always consistent activities, sometimes it made me tired or fed up but I never gave up but I gathered all my consistencies whenever I got frustration to go away from that frustration I used to go to maternal uncle's house, there was an bicycle which was purchased by my father for me, it gave me uncountable happiness, that cycle which was father's gift for me helped me as his bless and I regularly went for tuition and practical's on that bicycle only.

Those all activities narrated here to show my perseverance and consistency. I want to request to you too never fed up and never stop the continuity we should always proceed our job because

৩

VI

"A rolling stone gathers no moss"

2002 - 2003 (D. Ed.) City of glamour :

After 12th I never stopped my educational journey and it doesn't deserve to stop a little ant also struggle for better future so why we should not literally we are learner from first day till last day of our life. I returned home after 12th at Deola and took admission for B.Sc. I run and fro or daily travel by bus after few month, I went Mumbai D. Ed. college of Mumbai. It was admittance in D. Ed. college of Mumbai. It was my dream city. I was admitted in 'Vanita Vinaylaya D. Ed. College Girgaon, Mumbai. My elder sister was also passed from there and it was my time I took my entry. One more joyful occurrence which made my father delighted was my admission at Mumbai here Mumbai means positive experience in Queen City. I reached in a hostel I never ever seen this kind of humanistic place in my life, our supertendent Miss Lata Shah was very well mannered and admirable lady. We used to go college by walk or some times we hire BEST bus no.64, from hostel. I believed on simple living high thinking because I was aware about glamour of Mumbai but knew.

"Simplicity is the best fashion."

I wore simple Punjabi dress after a while I realized that there the appearance of jeans and t-shits is high lifestyle although appearance deceptive but it was needed in that glamour city for good standard of living I also changed myself improved my communication skills as well as my appearance I bought new dresses, night dresses, jeans, tops, t-shirts other glamorous and necessary equipments and garments. My D.Ed. College was an English medium D.ed. College, maximum students belonged to high profile family we enjoyed a lot there because it only girls college.

Our Sudha miss, Kor miss and other are unforgettable their teaching strategies, co-operative behaviour and enthusiastic capabilities, How can one forget I began to realize how important it to be an enthusiast in life..........

Environment or atmosphere of hostel was really spiritual and calm. Our morning schedule used to start prayer, Geyser warm water facility provided in each bathroom we used bath daily but you know about basic instinct of hostel to have a bath was also like task there but I awake early in the morning and would complete this task hostel also provided us food it was hygienic, delicious and nutritious vegetarian food was provided, only two three girls were pursuing D. Ed. there including but others MBBS, CA, BAMS, Engineering Diploma, Degree, B.Sc., M.Sc., Architecture and preparation for staff selection exam (SSC), CGL and many different courses which helped me a lot as I told you I am learner, I learnt a lot by their courses while they studied I also used to study with them I helped me very much. Now my success is followed my hostel experience. It improved my communication skills and development. I always recall my remarkable friends among them one of my dearest Seematai who helped me because she was my senior. I learnt thousands of new thermo and real philosophy of our life we only blow in our own trumpet for very short time, trust me I saw thousands of different kinds of people in my life they were disagreed with my simple nature I changed my nature my kind hearted activities because I believe on immortal activities and heard,

"Once the game is over, the
King and the Pawn go back
In the same box."
ITALIAN PROVERB

VII
Metaphorical journey

2003 - 2004 Beginning of career :

After the golden age of dream city (Mumbai) I returned from light glamour to small town Chandwad it was a very small village. I worked there as an English medium school teacher at S.N.J.B, English Medium School Chandwad. It was my first experience as an employee I used to run and fro from Umrane to Chandwad by school bus every day a lot means I was a lot fond of teaching. I used to prepare lesson plan my daily jotting. Students were from Umrane came every evening to me for tuition that schedule and hard work gave me satisfaction. In our school, there were many programme were celebrated, events and extra curricular / co curricular activities were organized mostly our class conquered prizes among all classes. We would try our best for winner prestige.

I taught there only 06 months but in that duration I improved very much my teaching style. I left S.N.J.B. Chandwad and appointed at K. D. Bhalerao School

Lakhamapur as preprimary teacher believe me when I was appointed I didn't know it will become my final destination. I saw there at Lakhamapur really need of improvement of students so tried my best I started there with basic, quality education at the beginning I only guided and gave them knowledge regarding small letters, poems, rhyme, verse, stories among those all things they were fond of stories which told by me. Although they had an affection with the stories which were told to them by me but my real story, my genuine story was still in the struggle. I used to come school by government bus in those days it was quite difficult I strived a lot but never broke my consistency. Our team K.D.B. teachers tried our best to make them clever/intelligent. Now they tribal students needed only proper guidance and specific direction. I told everything to my father and he became very happy. I continued my curricular and extracurricular activities. We organized demonstration programme also and those programmes made tribal locality parents very happy. Sometimes rarely if I reached school not on time students used to wait for me and became happy after looking me.

I not only used to concentrate my brilliant students but also my average students were concentrated by me. Once altogether we have visited at Pahadeshwar temple as field trip. It was delightful beginning of career.

VIII
Delightful Days

2004 - 2005 :

My career and grapple was running parallel but in that struggle one of the biggest accomplishment my life and it was my marriage. Although it was a court marriage yes, on 23rd December there was my court marriage with Mr. Sharad Bhalerao. I am a lady who believe on a one man woman theory firstly he proposed me and I agree to marry with him.

"एक वचन माझ्याकडून जेवढे सुख देता येईल तेवढे देईल,
काहीही झाले तरी मी शेवटपर्यंत साथ मात्र तुला देईल."

Several episode we faced before and after marriage in fact my parents were agreed but my Jiju (brother - in - law) and 3rd number sister both of them not admitting that marriage. I couldn't realize why they were not agreed even though we both belongs to prestigious families. I am also Hindu Maratha and he is also Hindu Kunbi here is no question of inter caste marriage but somehow in our family many other members met each other to solve that foolish question but answer was still negative even people tried a lot to crack that programme but they failed because It was my desire to marry with him and I used to achieve specially what my ambition is and my ambition was to marry with this good natured man honestly today I also like his calm behaviour, his comfortable friendly supportive communication style, his kindness, his lovable personality.

"थी मैं एक बेनाम सितारा,
मेरी असल पहचान हो तुम ।
खुदा ने जो उसकी इबादत पर मुझे दी,
मेरी मन्नत का इनाम हो तुम ।
अपने हर जनम में जिसे पाना चाहूँ
वो अनमोल उपहार हो तुम,
भर दो ये सुनी माँग मेरी
मेरा सारा संसार हो तुम ।

Both we determined and agreed to marry in the court on 23rd December 2004 at Malegaon we married with delightfulness. I was happy and little bit sad also because I left my parents though I was ready for any situation, already I set up my mind to fight with several difficulties and time had arisen so after marriage we went at Tai's house who is sir' sister we call her 'Tai' auspiciously she acted us merrily next day when my father-in-law and mother-in-law came there they told me,

"We have two daughters and your now our third daughter from today,"

I was very happy because one joyful moment means acceptance followed by one. One of our brother's-in-law and didi didn't accept us only it was a problem but it was burden some time for my husband also it was very hard for us because my family totally had left me and very few members of his family were accepting.

Since then till now I am totally depend upon his decisions. I left happily my family for him to look his supportive attitude he has proved loyalty hundreds of times according to

"हजारो नाते असतील पण त्या
हजार नात्यात एक असे नाते,
जे हजार नाते विरोधात असताना **सुद्धा**
सोबत असते **ती** म्हणजे बायको."

As I have promised that I am always with you (Bhalerao sir), so untilled I will die I will hold his hand. It's my promise apropos I was totally unaware about his family I didn't know anything about them so sometimes I faced loveless ness situation. I never quit between 23rd December to 31st December we stayed at Tai's house and on 1st of January New Year we came at sir's it means our sweet home. My brother-in-law used to fight with my sister-in-law on some topic. I was too much scared because in my family (maternal) I had never seen such kinds of quarrel from next day means 2nd January only I started adjustment with them I dwelt it was tough for me. I was even unfamiliar by making Chapati even I didn't know its processes, Sabji and other house chores were quite difficult for me I tried to do my best and over-come too. I want to share here my personal experience with you that marriage means nothing only marry with a man. It is a task to handle whole family including bridegroom. My sweet husband, my supportive husband helped me and by blessing and grace of God and with assistance of high power Almighty I kept going not only house chores but also school works. I continued it any situation but never forgot my maternal family, parents although I was very busy in my work but gave real affection and provided love as possible as pure everyone but couldn't get same affection same love same purity return, adulteration found.

Just because of that fondness my thirst or my hunger for love from my side especially for changed into lack affection and this malpractice made my nature negative.

Real or fake?
"Food adulteration is new trend
Water is mixed with mik.
Artificial colours are added to fruits
What one can expect from people."
Anupreksha Jain

Every person is not good or exactly like our expectation. I helped those people as well who refused to help me. It was reason of my nervousness apart from that nervous feelings my husband who used to give time to his college always tried to handled me, his work and our family. He had provided me all the necessary things balanced every episode of our life story really such a brave personality.

On 10th June 2005 we were going to celebrate a reception at my house which was entirely prepared by my husband. People gathered to attend it. I tried for my parents but they denied. I again became very sad. I thought it was our own decision which both of us had taken. Our marriage and it is possibilities depend upon people to accept us or to refuse us number of relatives, friends, dignitaries of the society came to attend it. We enjoyed and I not only saw but me also several people who were known as stars of the society in those days they celebrated our programme. One unpleasant thing that my brother-in-law and didi were unhappy with my decision to overcome from that situation it was really very difficult for me.

After all the celebration when we started our family and future discussion then we decided to nourish or nurture our 30 students' school into the best school in Maharashtra state. We finally decided to start new struggle strategy for new admissions solaceful news we succeed nearly one hundred new boys and girls I got these new tasks, I also got new burden of my personal and professional duties.

My professional life was not difficult rather than my personal life but thank God I never felt apprehension only I faced problems without afraid and always defeated all illusions. Probably I adopted different points of views. Some time I lost my strength of life but always thought that a supernatural power of God is behind me who enhance or improve me. I tried and tried but changed and learnt.

"If you think you are beaten,
You are.
If you think you dare not,
You don't.
If you would like to win but think,
You can't.
If you think you will lose,
You have lost.
Life is battles don't always go, to
The stranger or faster man;
But to the man who is certain he can.
(WALTER D WINTLE)

IX

One side Samarth another side establishment of school

2005 - 2006 :

"It is not the strongest of the species that survives, nor the most intelligent that survives. It is the one that is most adaptable to change."

· **Charles Darwin**

I understand life is nothing but its another name is replace, probably I adopted different points of views I knew everything about cruelty of time, knew very well behaviour of, time, also know 'time and tide wait for none' nut I continued my obligations but end we overcame from an abstract obstacle really we conquered the admission

mission but task was stilled in front of us it was nothing but the development of our students we were to bring up or to keep running hurry up our K.D.B. school there were only 02/03 teachers with me. K.G. and 1st class were in school. We shifted our school at sir's (Bhalerao) friends Sadashiv Bhamare's land, he gave us it on rent, and we regularly paid as rent. We had constructed there temporary school building with plants, greenery, flowers, nursery made it happy school. I think now a days we felt strong there due to a very small but strong Ganpati temple was near our school so bravely we handled students. I had run out of patients because I wanted to solve all problems of the society altogether but I forgot that

"Rome was not built in a day."

We conducted our 1st Annual day function celebrated with several dances, dramas, cultural activities, all activities that function were choreographed by me I helped my those super 30 students with honesty and they we really 30 students some solo dances, few dramas were very unusual and very nice and familiar for example Dhoom Machade, Dhangar vadyat those kind of activities were presented with full energy and sprightly by us. Dr. Kamal Aher became the master of ceremony (emcee) he abbreviated at our innumerous activities that time but it was Annual Function and Dr. Kamal Aher one of the best, he was the anchor of our first Annual function honestly 1st Annual function is memorable for us and after few months I begot a son. I generated a baby boy and our new born baby's name we kept 'Samarth' means able, capable, competent here 'Samarth Bhalerao' is my expectation, it was happiest moment for us to give birth to a boy is like our hopes, desires. On 15th of October 2005 both we firstly treated by Dr. Nikhil Sonawane's hospital. In those day my paternal or maternal families did not look after me but Bhalerao sir's family means my son's paternal family looked after me in those days too they handled and co-operated me a lot that's why I used to present my gratitude to them because

"A STITCH IN TIME

SAVES NINE."

And they looked after me very well although it was normal delivery but I was well treated by them. My sister-in-law (Kalpana) used to provide me food on time, my mother-in-law, my husband and others co-operated me every guest used to come to meet us in those happy days. I missed my parents in that difficult time but unfortunately they were not with me and instead of them my husband and my family members were with me. I am really lucky regarding specially my husband and family which became mine. Although today I am very brave and combative lady like Mary Kom but when I was needy they hold my hands. It we have been hurt many times, and we stilled know how to smile, it means we are strong. Yes I am flexible in nature, I faced every types of situations and I won lastly whatever situation we should face and finally it will OK never give up on a dream just because of situation or time it will take to accomplish it, situation or time will pas anyway. Day's were being passed and my son Samarth was growing day after day. I used to talk, laugh and used to enjoy with him. I though God sent a wonderful toy for me to play. I'll call it my golden era not only me but my husband also love him a lot he used to bring noteworthy toys as token of love for him even today also we are using those things which he has brought for him in those days believe me those are today also useful. My husband can handle college, family and friends altogether properly but it was quite difficult for me in those days but not now I want to be like him I hope I will success.

"ऐसे अनेक **पुत्र** किस काम के
जो दुःख और निराशा पैदा करे
इससे तो वह एक ही **पुत्र** अच्छा है
जो पुरे घर को सहारा और शांति प्रदान करे."

चाणक्य

X

School having resemblance to Battlefield

2006 to 2010 :

Our first priority is our K.D.B we accustomed to think about our school. I used to discuss with my husband about the developed of K.D.B. I adopted new family and school staff family. We used to try or we have been trying our best for quality education and usually we spend our quality time in productivity we have started numerous productive works in our school. In all my devotion, dedication, wholeheartedness. I worked with my team for betterment of our nation, out motherland now any vision had expanded I not only used to think about school, family or society but also nation wide and world wide although I have some silly nuisance of the society to which probably disappointed me for a while but I let it go I never upset because I know an angry mind is a narrow mind. I only was unhappy due to my parents I wanted to meet them, I missed them very much but I couldn't, I loved my parents and missed too only parents didn't miss other relatives even sisters because I was their beloved and I wanted to talk with them about my aim yes including all these emotional I had a professional part of my life as well I made my life busy to get the aim my aim was my school its progress my all movements were towards achieving my goals. During day as well as at night we use to work my teaching staff had done several productive activities for success of our school because it is a part of our life. At that time till the school came on its track I was also fully settled in my family often relatives and guests to and froed at home. We used to cook new and delicious food for them. School was also running on its proper style. Instantly I got an innovative idea, immediately it was implemented by me and it was our Educational Exhibition for development, enhancement the inner qualities of my students. We made several projects, all teachers helped model making according to their subject and their topic which was given to them. It was literally an initiative for me I nearly solved all my problems after that initiative I organized numerous events like our great magnificent Independence Day function and Republic Day celebration, projects other festivals programme, sport activities, different exhibitions and Annual function etc. we had celebrated enthusiastically and countless pursuits. Now school become an essential part of our life. One of the most important factors in all those achievements are none of other but only the hard work of my school teachers my team and my school parents too. Happiness of those parents were our rewards. Teachers always obeyed the Principal's orders and it was the key of my success there many obstacles were also presented on my path but my school teachers who listened and implemented whatever order passed by ma'am their obedient behaviour was my real achievement.

Although I started my journey with very small shed, small ground, a small Ganapati temple but I firmly believed hard work, struggle, persevering, and endeavor.

I knew Quote of (SWAMI VIVEKANANDA)

"ARISE, AWAKE AND STOP NOT

TILL THE GOAL IS REACHED"

Swami Vivekananda

Those events are unforgettable for me. I proceeded in my battle like Rajmata Jijau, Rani Lakshmibai, Savitribai Phule, Pandita Ramabai, Mother Teresa and Ramabai Ranade.

XI

Consummating of the Desires

2010 - 2018 :

I got going my prosperous job and attainment. Our struggle was then had changed into a ripened fruit. We then understood that we were on right path we purchased new land for school and we started new building construction but it was with extra facilities such as library, conference hall, computer lab, indoor hall, art gallery room, science lab, program auditorium, lunch place for students even thought it is a building for others but for us its our dream project.

**"DREAM is not what you see in
Sleep,
DREAM is something which doesn't
Let you sleep."
Dr. A. P. J. Abdul Kalam**

So our dream project was fully planned with complete facilities though was strategic planning by Mr. Sharad Bhalerao sir and me. Really it is not simply school it is my final destination. Only in the duration of 02/03 years our school chairman sir made a complete infrastructure of school. Our motive of the dream was to provide all the facilities to our dear students we will never know our limits until we push ourselves to them and great people also have advised us such a wonderful truth such as

"The great secret of true success,
Of true happiness, is this?
The man or woman who asks for
No return.
The perfectly unselfish person is the
Most successful."

· **Swami Vivekananda**

though we got going our work in unselfish manner it was being planned for and creative things in our school such as English lab, Talking pen, Worksheets, Talking chart, debate competition, Math's Abacus and like those many wonderful activities.

Guest lectures by expertise have been inviting for motivation of our pupils, one more thing that whenever we organized any motivational lecture o any psychiatrist or expertise we could feel instant result and positive changes in our pupils. We used to try to present our deepest gratitude from our bottom of the heart to our Lord Almighty God please to protect us from devil eyes or nuisances.

परित्राणाय साधूनां विनाशाय च दुष्कृताम् ।
धर्मसंस्थापनार्थाय संभवामि युगे युगे ॥८॥

Bhagavad Gita: Chapter 4, Verse 8.

**"Paritranaya Sdhunam Vinashaya cha dushkritam
Dharm-sansthapnarthya Sambhavami Yuge Yuge"
Its translation
"To protect the righteous, to annihilate
The wicked,
And to reestablish the principles of
Dharma I appear on this earth, age
After age."**

For the social health of our students we organized many events, festival celebrations, seminar, interschool competitions etc. Even though we completely dedicated for pupils even economically, mentally, physically entirely just for their development for a while we ignored our family but we never compromised with school. It simply our scarification that we have given 100 % to our school. I really transparent and fair in my all judgments, I don't know what 'Bias' is, while giving quality education we don't consider some one as rich or some one as poor, neither we classify in rural – urban nor in cast or creed. We are fully transparent in our judgments with boys and girls relation or religion. We are away from gender bias and stereotype. We only used to do our spiritual and divine services for the welfare of our students, no partiality and no bias stereotype we try to justify with transparency in prize distribution and in appreciation also.

As earlier I narrated that,

"Rome was not built in a day." It's absolutely right but here my work was in progress and still going on but I firmly believe on

"Slow and steady wins the race."

My perseverance, my consistency my hard work and my continuity proved my capabilities. I have been working as a Principal and awarded as the Best Principal award. I made possible to all impossible tasks although it's quite difficult to handle students, all teachers, society, parents, family, economy and one of the most important things our dignity and our self respect altogether but my school result and our school prestige shows our inner qualities that we are real warriors and true soldiers in all battlefields and our strength is our innovative ideas and your love and respect.

XII

Solace in the suffering

2018 - 2020 :

My story was going towards happy endings subsequently each situation was under control I was extremely pleased due to pregnancy news I was really delighted because Dr. Suvarna Pawar my friend was treating me. She recommend me about baby and date of delivery as 25th June, days passed and the sun of that day was to move upwards that complex and unforgettable day it was truly a composite unexplainable day that I had to face cesarean delivery the operation or surgical delivery and its treatment was based on 07 days those burdensome 07 day are most memorable days in my life because at that time who chores were came altogether one was accouchement and another task or responsibility of my Niraj. It was painful time for me although birth of Niraj made me happy but his left leg's foot was somehow curved so I was very anxious I lost my all strength it made me very nervous we eagerly went to doctors but Dr. Suvarna Pawar gave me solace and motivation simultaneously I had two pains one my physical which was tolerable but my son's left leg was curved that one sentence even was intolerable for me. It gave me pain, I lost my strength.

Dr. Dipak Pawar, Pediatric. Yes he could be doctor for others but for us he is metaphorical magician. Dr. Dipak Pawar, Pediatric Surgeon suggested us for foot surgery under the treatment of Chhalawar doctor.

An infant was going to face an operation you can imagine how painful and burdensome situation we have faced but we used to tell our – self be brave it was a surgery and the pain which he had to bear only he could understand we wanted to share his pain but we couldn't share and my son bore himself he proved himself as a warrior and son of the warrior, among all these talk one of the most important points Did you notice? Here real warrior is my husband who played a very very important role in my operation and my son's operation he is self – discipline, long-term goal achiever, self regulation willpower personality strongly fought and defeated all nuisances. He used to go to change the plaster of my infant every week. 01 ½ years treatment of my Niru was going on but he did it with consistency. I am very lucky that this kind of willpower personality is behind me. I used to pray God protect him honestly that treatment was hectic for us because Niru had to wear shoes during night as well doctor suggested to use night tight shoes, he had given painful reaction but it was for his good health. We know that but how to tell him. he was on breastfeeding and that tight shoes so it was quite difficult for him to suck the milk or to get right position so often I didn't sleep at night I used to pick up him up an fed during day or night I had to handle school and my Niru specially at night. My physical health, body, mind was not supporting me I felt imbalance sometime went out of my control. Finally I made schedule including night upto morning 07:00 a.m. I was handling and I was looking after him bur from morning 07:00 a.m. to evening 07:00 p.m. Shubhangi looked after him, she used to do her duty honestly. Shubhangi was skilled in her work one caretaker Mavshi also used to help her it was consolation me. My only solace that God doesn't leave me alone always sends any Angel or Fairy to help me, Shubhangi and me, we helped each others, but her help is not can be measure money yet it is noteworthy or significant.

"The strongest people make time to help others,
Even they are struggling with their own problems."

BIODATA

Name: Mrs. Tanaya Sharad Bhalerao
Education:
D.Ed. (Mumbai)
M.A. B.Ed.
Address: Post: Lakhamapur, Taluka: Satana,
District: Nashik
Pin code: 423213
Birth date: 23-03-1984
Vice Chairman, K.D. Bhalerao Education Society
Post: Professor, K.D. Bhalerao English Medium School
and Junior College, Lakhamapur.
Phone No: 02555-235770
Mob No: 9168216070 / 9890718070

Social Activities and Integration:

- Financial assistance for widows (Vidhashray Sanstha)
- Presenting gratitude by distributing Diwali clothes and faral with Gram Panchayat cleaning staff.
- Offered Free health check up and treatment for women.
- Helping financially poor students for free education.
- Disability Day honored by providing financial assistance to the disabled.
- Conducting school health camps for girls.
- Conducting karate training camps for girls for self defense.

THANKS BY (I)

Sharad Bhalerao chairman of Lakhamapur international school going to congratulate to the principal of bhalerao education society for debut her book. She is Mrs. Bhalerao but she considers herself first principal of English medium school lakhamapur. Yes, I overlook and read also her book and want to appreciate her cause she has been working from initial and with great appropriateness. Yes I am witness of her every events but I am astonished that even she has very busy schedule than also she has written this wonderful book which shows her struggle, manner diligent activities, wisdom, flowery days adventurous events, incomparable long suffering but magnificent victory.

Her strength, struggle and her continuous fight unable to express by any book but she tried with modification work and conquer.

Lastly behalf of L.E.M.S teachers and reputed members I again congratulate her for her awe- inspiring, interesting, enjoyable charming, and visionary book.

- Sharad Bhalerao

THANKS BY (II)

I didn't know and I couldn't know her importance until I read her dignified stories but I understood now their admirable activities and absolutely pure aptitude talent, skills.

I don't have words in front of her powerful description but I congratulate her and express my deepest gratitude for this book. I read it now once but I'll hold it whole life.

Thank you mom, you are such an unbeatable super woman tanaya bhalerao.

- Samarth Bhalerao

৪০

Thanks By (III)

To be an unbreakable member of K.D.B. family, its prideful moment for me that my honorable principal is going to publish a book named "Words of Life". Yes me very lucky that mam has given me a chance to overlook this book. She has shared her many events with KBD teachers. I hope and we pray that almighty Rab our God always make her delightful, prosperous and her achievement and success may illuminate with bright shining like stars and moon.

Yes I read this book and going to say thank to our principal Tanaya Bhalerao for publish this motivational book for us.

\- NAZIM KHAN
Asst. teacher, KBD

Thanks By (iv)

People consider that it is happy ending and she is happily living with her both son's somarth and niru, havinf substantially glorious life but her struggling is still in progress only direction has changed.

now she is living her life still with hard working for all the children of nation to be a good mother, good wife, good sister, good daughter, good principal, good friend, good guide, good human being, good indian as she told her story is not her story only, it's a story of every girl.

- Everyone.
- Every body.

Bibliography Of Words Of Life

Words of life is not only the story of Tanaya Bhalerao's life but it is a story of all women who showing grapple, struggling, ongoing, continuing fight for happiness and long suffering with technique and creativity but showing mercy, generosity, loyalty and captivating great beauty with positive tolerance and forgiving. In this book leading character - Tanaya Bhalerao faced problems during study, migration problem join family of her father and then after her glamorous hostel life surprising events and emotional as well as desirous incidents of life. It shows our Indian tradition that how a girl shows variations, diversity and how she lives her life with adaptation and boldness. If they use their illuminator courage they can get triumph, victory or conclusive success in their life.

Although she did her school and family work equally in parallel way but how her trust worthy husband came in her life as an angel so after every fight her life became prestigious, unable splendid and refreshing.

Book gives us a message at the end which is a proverb.

"No matter how long the winter,

Spring is sure to follow."

www.ingramcontent.com/pod-product-compliance
Lightning Source LLC
Chambersburg PA
CBHW052232150726
48002CB00003B/1391